The Road to
Happiness
Is Always
Under Construction

50 Activities for
Creating a Positive Outlook

K. Je

Foreword

D1445539

Robert D. Reed Publishers   •   Bandon, OR

Robert D. Reed Publishers
P.O. Box 1992
Bandon, OR 97411
Phone: 541-347-9882; Fax: -9883
E-mail: 4bobreed@msn.com
Website: www.rdrpublishers.com

Editor: Cleone Reed
Cover Designer: Cleone Reed
Front cover photo: Road to Skye © Tonyd from dreamstime.com
Artist: Debby Gwaltney
Book Designer: Debby Gwaltney

ISBN 13: 978-1-934759-45-5
ISBN 10: 1-934759-45-7

Mixed Sources
Product group from well-managed forests and other controlled sources
www.fsc.org   Cert no. SW-COC-002283
© 1996 Forest Stewardship Council

FSC

Library of Congress Control Number: 2009943827

Manufactured, Typeset, and Printed in the United States of America

Table of Contents

Dedication

To My Sister Pam

Acknowledgments

No one ever writes a book alone. All books are a compellation of the people we have met, the people we know, and the experiences we share. Like so many authors I have had the privilege of meeting and knowing many wonderful people as I have traveled the road to happiness.

Thanks and praise to my wife Kim and our children Ben, Andy, Emily, and Katie. Thank you for your love and support. I love you very much and I am always proud of you.

Thanks to Steve Chandler. Steve, you are a true hero to me. Your championing of this work has lead to the opportunity of a lifetime for me as a writer. You even went a step further by writing the foreword. How gracious! I am eternally grateful for your help and contribution.

Thanks to my best friend Dr. Dan Bowersox. Dan, your friendship and support in this project have been invaluable. I love you like a brother.

Thanks to Dr. Lou Sportelli, Dr. Jim Anderson, and Dr. Rodger Tepe. Gentlemen, your encouragement and comments on the initial manuscript helped me move forward. I am honored by your friendship.

Thanks to Robert Reed, Cleone Reed, Debby Gwaltney and everyone at Robert Reed Publishing for your professionalism and hard work. You have provided a wonderful experience.

Lastly, to those from my life who played a role in this narrative, thank you for the experiences we shared and the opportunity to tell the stories.

Foreword

The construction of our happiness is a project we usually leave to others. We want *other people* to make us feel happy and safe and fulfilled. We look outside ourselves for our happiness, and it never seems to fully arrive. And even when we do receive some appreciation and love, we never know whether to trust it.

Because we are looking in the wrong place. We are barking up the wrong tree. Other people aren't the answer.

This book can get us over to the right tree. Dr. Jeff Miller has given us a construction guide that contains fifty brief and understandable steps. Inspiring steps, too! Steps that add one elemental piece of happiness at a time, in a witty conversational style. It's also full of fun stories and absolutely great quotes.

I especially like his chapter about planning his own funeral. After attending the funeral of his father, and observing how many tedious arrangements are involved in such an activity, he decides he doesn't want his family to go through the same thing when *he* dies. So he goes back to the mortuary and plans everything out for his own death so it's all taken care of.

Not only does this eliminate procrastination, but it also gives our author a fresh, clear sense of his own mortality. Life on earth is brief! Let's get on with the show! If you have goals it's time to turn them into *projects*!

It's time to live.

These fifty construction steps are the perfect antidotes for those of us who tend to put off living and wait for good fortune to arrive from somewhere else. Somewhere like the future.

As you read through one step after another you start to feel the momentum building for a call to continuous action. This book gives you things to *do*, not just things to think about.

In his chapter on our ultimate time-waster, the negative mainstream media, Dr. Miller concludes with these unforgettable words: "You cannot save time. Time can only be wasted or spent wisely."

That was one of the many passages my yellow highlighter has marked for future reading. *Time can only be wasted or spent wisely.* That's the message I take from this book.

Reading this book on how to construct happiness is time spent wisely. Especially now when so many of the books in the human performance and "self-help" field are absolute wastes of time! Books about the law of attraction in which you learn to become passive and close your eyes and dream of a far-off future. Books about "attracting" wealth. Books that feed on people's hopes and dreams.

This book does the opposite. It opens your eyes and feeds on your love of action. It returns the power to you. It shows you how to *build* happiness, rather than waiting for it to occur.

And in my favorite touch, Dr. Miller's last chapter asks you to read his book again. I loved that! Why should we believe in a book that does not believe in itself? Believe in this book. And you will really know how good it is by reading it a second time and taking the steps it gives you.

Steve Chandler
Phoenix, Arizona
November, 2009

Introduction

"There is no happiness; there are only moments of happiness."
Spanish proverb

I am not an optimistic person. I am melancholy and pessimistic by nature. I can see the gloom and doom in almost anything. I have always been this way. Whether this is genetic or environmental, I don't know. It does, however, seem to run in my family.

The good news: I realize this and work to balance my thoughts, moods, and outlook. I say "balance" instead of "correct" because I have found that my nature is not completely correctable. It can be improved, but it requires continued maintenance in order to keep me from reverting to my melancholy pessimistic ways.

Improvements and maintenance are achieved through motivational books, audio/video/DVD programs, and seminars. Goal-oriented activities are also a tremendous help. Nothing perks me up more than the achievement of a goal, large or small. Pursuing goals keeps me busy and occupies my mind. This leaves less time for worry.

Are you pessimistic too? Do you need to balance your thoughts, moods, and outlook? If you are, then this book is for you. It contains many of the ideas and activities I have used to control my pessimistic melancholy nature.

My hope is that it *will not* be a motivational book that inspires you temporarily and then leaves you hanging. You know what I mean—words that tell you everything is going to be fine but do not give you the tools and actual activities needed to help you help yourself.

This book is about action. The activities here require work on your behalf. Each of the chapters focuses on an idea/activity that you can work on over the course of a few weeks. Once the idea/activity is in progress or complete, you quickly move on to the next one. By the time you work your way through the book, life will be better. You will feel more accomplished and prepared.

Some of the activities are long term or on-going. Others are started and finished in a short period of time. Maintaining the on-going activities and working toward goals will help keep your mind off negative thoughts and also elevate your mood. The short-term events can be repeated later if you choose. Short-term items are good for jump-starting your mind and elevating your mood when you need a quick boost.

If you are not melancholy or pessimistic by nature, you can still use this book. The activities are good for anyone. Nobody is up twenty-four/seven. We all feel a little down in the dumps occasionally.

In *Curing a Cold* (1863) Mark Twain wrote, *"It is a good thing, perhaps, to write for the amusement of the public, but it is a far higher and nobler thing to write for their instruction, their profit, their actual and tangible benefit."*

I echo this sentiment. It is my hope that this writing will add to the resources currently available for improving the lives of my fellow man, pessimist or optimist. All be it, I doubt I will achieve this with the same degree of humor exhibited by Twain.

Make it happen!

Dr. K. Jeffrey Miller

01 Get Stressed Out

> 66 You never will be the person you can be if pressure, tension, and discipline are taken out of your life. 99
>
> ~ *James G. Bilkey*

Americans frequently talk about being "stressed-out" and the need to "reduce stress." They talk about stress like it is a bad thing. You are probably saying, "It is a bad thing!" Not necessarily. Stress has gotten a bad rap over the last few decades.

Stress isn't all bad. There are actually two types of stress, distress and eustress. Both types represent challenges to body and mind, but one is bad and one is good.

Distress is bad stress, stress that causes wear and tear on the body, anxiety and an emotional toll on the mind. Injury and illness, overtime, malnutrition, divorce, job loss, and debt are examples. Distress is destructive and detrimental.

Eustress is good stress, stress that causes the body and mind to respond by becoming stronger. Exercise, studying, and goal setting are examples. Eustress results in improvements and advancements.

I once brought up the subject of eustress to a psychologist I know. She appeared puzzled at first and said she did not know the word. The next time I saw her she said she had looked up the word and was somewhat embarrassed that I had known the term and she had not. She admitted that over the years she had become so focused on dealing with her patients' distress that she had simply forgotten about eustress. Even mental health professionals get caught in the stampede of bad stress. Obviously, we all need more eustress.

When distress outweighs eustress, life is bad. When distress and eustress are equal, life is stagnant. When eustress outweighs distress, life is good.

The activities described in this book are eustress activities. Do them all!

02 You Are Smarter Than You Think

> 66 When I stand before God at the end of my life, I would hope that I would not have a single bit of talent left, and I could say, 'I used everything you gave me.' 99
>
> ~ *Erma Bombeck*

We have all taken standardized tests. Achievement tests, placement tests, entrance tests, and IQ tests are common during our scholastic years. For some these tests were proud moments while for others they were drudgeries. If they were drudgeries for you there is good news.

The truth about intelligence is there is more than one type. In fact, over a hundred types have been described. According to the book, *7 Kinds of Smart* by Thomas Armstrong, research has consistently shown seven of these intelligences are particularity common. The seven types of intelligence are linguistic, logical-mathematical, spatial, musical, bodily kinesthetic, interpersonal, and intrapersonal.

Standardized tests only test for linguistic intelligence, the use of words. So, if you don't do well on standardized tests there is no reason to feel stupid. You may be a genius in one or more of these six intelligences.

Linguistic Intelligence: the intelligence of words

Logical-mathematical Intelligence: the use of reasoning and numbers

Spatial Intelligence: intelligence in pictures and images

Musical Intelligence: intelligence in rhythm and melodies

Bodily-kinesthetic Intelligence: intelligence in athletes, mechanics, and crafts

Interpersonal Intelligence: the intelligence of working with people

Intrapersonal Intelligence: intelligence of the inner self and self-discipline

We all have some degree of each type of intelligence; some predominate and some are deficient, but they are all present. Additional good news is each of the seven major types of intelligences can be developed and improved.

Tests are available that can identify your intellectual strengths. Career counselors and mental health professionals offer them. Take advantage of these tests. They can help you realize your true genius and direct you toward goals, activities, and careers that will allow your star to shine.

CHAPTER 03
Identify Your Personality

> 66 God, our creator has stored within our minds and personalities, great strength and ability. Prayer helps us tap and develop these powers. 99
>
> ~ *Abdul Kalam, President of India, 1931*

"You have no personality." That is the advice of Steve Chandler in the introduction to his book, *100 Ways to Motivate Yourself: Change Your Life Forever.* The point he makes with this statement is that we are all a work in progress and our personalities evolve as we do. I think he is partially right. We are works in progress, but we all have a core personality that influences the path we take in our development.

Using a map to determine the route to your future isn't possible if you do not know your starting point. You must know your starting point in order to arrive at your desired destination.

According to the Myers-Briggs Type Indicator System, there are four pairs of personality preferences. We possess a preference in each category. This means we possess more than one type of personality just as we possess more than one type of intelligence. Combinations of the four preferences result in sixteen possible personality types.

Your personality is a combination of one of the items from each of these pairs: Extroverted or Introverted, Sensing or Intuitive, Thinking or Feeling, and Judging or Perceiving. Each of these personality preferences has specific traits. They are the strengths and weaknesses you possess in multiple aspects of everyday life.

Investing the time and money in completing the Myers-Briggs Type Indicator will help you find your starting point on the map to your future. Otherwise, if you don't know from where you are starting, you cannot get to where you are going.

I took the Myers-Briggs Type Indicator when I was forty years old. By that time I had already identified many of the truths about my personality through the school of hard knocks. The test only confirmed my findings. I understood my personality. But I did regret the time and methods required to achieve this level of comfort. Had I taken the Myers-Briggs at a younger age, I could have avoided multiple hard-knock lessons.

Two of the best eustress activities you can participate in are identifying your dominant intelligences and personality. This will establish your starting point, destination, and the best possible path between the two.

CHAPTER 04 Win Where You Have Always Lost

> 66 Life does not consist in holding good cards
> but in playing a poor hand well. 99
>
> ~ *Thomas Fuller*

In the early 1990's I joined a business management firm for doctors. I joined because I was seeking help in building my practice; and after meeting the founder of the organization, Dr. David Kats, I knew it was the right decision. I eventually became a lifetime member and later a featured speaker for the organization for over a decade. I owe a lot to Dr. Kats. I learned a tremendous amount about business and life in general from him. This chapter and the next are about two related principles I learned from Dr. Kats.

In the early 90's I attended a seminar conducted by Dr. Kats. The title of one of the programs was "Win Where You Have Always Lost." The point of the lecture was that people often claim they are not good at something when actually they have no experience with the knowledge or activity in question. Obviously if someone has no experience in a particular area, it is logical that they would not be "good at it." On the other hand, there is no reason they cannot become good at it.

You really have no idea if you are good or bad at something until you have tried it. Even then if you have tried something and not been very good at it, you must ask yourself, "Did I stick with it long enough to be *good at it?*"

Maybe you have always wanted to play golf, play a musical instrument, act, write, or participate in some other activity but just could not bring yourself to try it. Go ahead and try anyway. The recommendation is to read a book, subscribe to a magazine, take lessons, or ask for help in an area you feel inadequate. Study and practice until you come to a point of decision; either you enjoy the endeavor and continue to improve or you decide it is not your cup of tea and move on. Virgil Thomson said,

> *"Try a thing you haven't done three times.*
> *Once, to get over the fear of doing it.*
> *Twice, to learn how to do it.*
> *And, a third time to figure out whether you like it or not."*

Maybe it is happiness you feel you are not good at. I've been there. By reading this book you are already on your way to learning more about happiness and *winning where you have always lost.*

05 *Ready, Fire, Aim*

> 66 Don't wait. The time will never be just right. 99
>
> ~ *Napoleon Hill*

Along the same lines of winning where you have always lost is the *ready-fire-aim* principle. The two principles are related in the fact that you hesitate to act until you think circumstances are perfect. You think you do not have the skill or knowledge to act. You may feel that circumstances must be perfect in order to avoid looking bad or failing.

The ready-fire-aim principle means you don't have to be good at something before you try it, and you must ignore your fear of looking bad or failing. Get ready, jump in there and do it; then adjust your aim and try again.

These principles along with the *win where you have always lost* philosophy have allowed me to attempt many activities I was interested in but would have avoided otherwise. Singing in a barbershop quartet, leaving private practice, and writing this book are examples.

Make fun of yourself as you go. Self-deprecating humor will help as you get started, and hang in there. Have fun with the process. Find someone else who is interested in the same activity and is just as inexperienced. Having a buddy will also help. You can lean on each other and learn together.

CHAPTER 06

Plan Your Funeral

> 66 Death is not the greatest loss in life.
> The greatest loss is what dies inside us while we live. 99
>
> ~ *Norman Cousins*
>
> 66 Have the courage to live. Anyone can die. 99
>
> ~ *Robert Cody*

My father died on May 7, 1997. The following day my sister and I accompanied our mother to the funeral home to make the funeral arrangement and purchase cemetery plots. This was a painful process. It became apparent early in the process that father had not discussed his last wishes with my mother in great detail. She had a difficult time making the necessary decisions in her acute grief. My mother seemed unsure of many of her decisions, and I could tell she worried if my father would have approved.

The funeral went well, but by the time it was over I had decided to plan my funeral the following week. I did not want my family to go through this process when I died. I went to the funeral home and planned everything. I selected a coffin and the music, pallbearers, burial sites, and other items. Funeral directors have a set of forms just for this process. Everyone but the funeral director thought I was crazy and the idea was morbid.

It may have been creepy for others, but it was very liberating for me. I was relieved that my family would not be forced to make difficult decisions during a time of grief and sorrow. I also had an opportunity to describe how I wanted to leave this world.

Most of all, I acknowledged that there is an end to my time on this earth. Admitting this helped me realize that there is a limited amount of time to accomplish my life's goals. This realization was a great inoculation against procrastination. The focus on my goals and dreams quickly increased. I had to get busy; the clock is ticking.

CHAPTER 07 Sing!

> 66 He who sings frightens away his ills. 99
>
> ~ *Miguel de Cervantes Saavedra, Spanish Writer*

William James said, "We do not sing because we are happy; we are happy because we sing." The old Johnny Cash tune *Daddy Sang Bass* says, "Daddy sang bass, momma sang tenor, me and little brother joined right in there; singing seems to help a troubled soul." And the Neil Diamond hit *Song Sung Blue* tells us, "Funny thing but you can sing it with a cry in your voice, and before your know it start to feeling good; you simply got no choice." Obviously, we should all sing more. Notice there is no mention of whether or not you can sing. It does not matter. It is what it does for you and not for others that matters.

Some of my earliest memories are of strumming a ukulele and singing for my parents, relatives, friends, and total strangers. I sang in chorus as a teenager. In my late thirties I sang in a barbershop quartet. I enjoyed all of these, and thankfully I could carry a tune. Singing has always brought me great joy, and in my darkest moments I have returned to it for comfort.

I did not always have a group to sing with, so I sang to myself. I turned up the car radio, tape or CD player, etc. and sang along. This never failed to elevate my mood. Eventually I made a cassette tape of my favorite songs to sing along with, and I play it when I am down or I want to get pumped up about something.

Make a tape or CD of your favorite music, play it, and sing along. Upload your I-Pod or MP3 Player with your favorites. Use the music to lift your spirits and to keep them up. Sing in the shower, in the car, or anywhere you can get away with it, even if you cannot carry a tune.

CHAPTER 08 Watch Jerry Springer

> 66 Gratitude changes the pangs of
> memory into a tranquil joy. 99
>
> ~ *Dietrich Bonhoeffer, German Theologian*

At this point you may be thinking the book is taking a turn for the worse. Watch Jerry Springer? How in the world could watching Jerry Springer help anything, especially your outlook in life? I know it is against classical motivational philosophy and it may seem mean, but seeing people who have more problems than you will elevate your mood. It is human nature.

I don't recommend this so you can gloat or make fun of the people who are guests of the "Worst Show in Television" (this is the show's slogan). I recommend it because after watching this show, almost everyone will realize their life isn't as bad as they thought. These poor people have screwed up their lives beyond belief—and then were crazy enough to go on national television to talk about it. And they don't just talk about it. They fight with each other, fight with the audience, strip, and do other bizarre things in the process.

Many say the whole thing is made up. It is a show like professional wrestling. I don't think so. I do think the show promotes some of the antics; but truth is stranger than fiction, and they have the market cornered on strange.

A friend of mine once told me his mother used to say, "I felt bad because I had no shoes until I met a man who had no feet." This saying tells you to be thankful for what you have. The Springer show is reality TV's version of saying the same thing.

Is it tacky? Yes! Is it white trash? Yes! But it works. Watch a couple of episodes and it will make you realize how good things really are in your life, and you will work to make sure you don't end up on national TV airing your dirty laundry and making a fool of yourself.

CHAPTER 09 *Save for Something*

> **"A penny saved is a penny earned."**
>
> ~ *Benjamin Franklin*

Have you ever had a piggy bank? I have! Actually it was not a piggy bank. It was a small metal bank in the shape of a globe. I can remember saving money in this bank for months to buy a fishing tackle box and later a baseball glove. As I aged I obtained my first savings account. Through middle school I saved for a drum set, college, and an engagement ring for the girl I would marry (even though I did not know who she would be at the time).

My parents taught me to save money. Ultimately this proved to be my first lesson in goal setting. I had something to look forward to, and I worked to obtain the money necessary to bring about what I wanted. The excitement of finally purchasing the items I saved for was tremendous.

I am afraid Americans have almost lost the ability to save for something we want or need. We live in a world of drive-through windows, credit cards, instant credit, payment plans, same-as-cash offers, and other instant conveniences. Why save for something when you can have it now?

Why? I'll tell you why—to learn goal setting, self-discipline, patience, and earn the self-respect that comes with finishing and goal completion. Not to mention the fact that when you pay later/on credit, you always pay more.

What do you save for? Save for needs and wants, small and large items, emergencies, college, and retirement. Just save!

To make this exercise practical you must select a couple of short-term savings goals. Saving for retirement is important, but the event is too far into the future to produce immediate positive effects. Save one thousand dollars for an emergency fund, and save for another item of five hundred dollars or less.

Dig out the old piggy bank and start a savings account. Start saving today, even if you owe money on your credit cards. If you wait until you are out from under other debts, you will never start. Get busy!

CHAPTER 10

Have a Hobby

> 66 Today is life-the only life you are sure of. Make the most of today. Get interested in something. Shake yourself awake. Develop a hobby. Let the wind of enthusiasm sweep through you. Live today with gusto. 99
>
> ~ *Dale Carnegie*

I used to ask my employees about their hobbies. I was especially interested to know if they collected a particular item. I wanted to know so when birthdays and Christmas came around, I could get them something they liked and wanted. All but one collected something. Spoons, Coke memorabilia, china dolls, baskets, and other items were among the collectables described. The one who said she did not collect anything informed me the day after I asked that she had started collecting Mercedes Benz cars. She then said she had not gotten the first one yet. "Nice try!" was my reply.

Hobbies and collectables bring joy and great pleasure to people. Unfortunately, many people do not have hobbies or have allowed hobbies to die because life is too busy. Work, the kids, keeping up with the Joneses, and other activities occupy all available time and suck the energy and life right out of them.

Take time to develop or rejuvenate a hobby. It can be something you share with friends or loved ones or something just for you. In fact, you could have one of each. This would double the benefits a hobby brings. You could take up ballroom dancing with your mate and starting collecting something just for yourself.

Hobbies do not have to be expensive or glamorous. I point to the spoon collection I mentioned above. They are the ones that are purchased at gift shops and truck stops. However, the spoons are just as meaningful as the expensive china dolls and baskets that my other employees collected. It is the meaning—not the financial value—that is important.

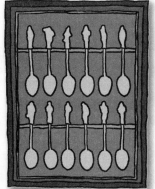

The other important point here is that your hobbies are your choice. Don't take on someone else's hobbies. It is fun to share hobbies, but make sure they are hobbies you are happy with.

CHAPTER 11

Fish Now

> 66 Retirement kills more people than hard work ever did. 99
>
> ~ *Malcolm S. Forbes*

Early in my chiropractic practice I went to lunch with Dr. Ronald Waldridge. He had treated my family as I was growing up. Initially, we chit chatted about how practice was going for me and other topics. Then he asked me what I liked to do. At the time I really did not have any hobbies or interests. I was so busy building a practice and raising a family I did not feel I had time for anything else.

Next he asked me what I wanted to do when I retired. Again, I didn't have a good answer. I could not tell where he was going with this line of questioning, and thankfully he stopped questioning me and made his point.

He told me that in over thirty years of practice he had watched countless patients die shortly after retiring. Most of them had worked hard all their lives and were waiting until retirement to pursue their dreams and favorite activities only to be foiled by illness and death.

Fishing, he related, was one of the most common things men seemed to look forward to in retirement. Then he addressed me directly saying, "If you want to fish, fish now." For Dr. Waldridge it was "hunt now."

I went on to practice almost seventeen years, and in that time I watched countless patients prove him right. It was amazing how many of my patients died shortly after retiring.

In Chapter 7 I recommended getting a hobby. Now I am telling you the hobby has to start now and continue. Don't wait!

I think the advice Dr. Waldridge gave me that day was some of the best advice I ever received from another doctor. Since that time I have tried several different hobbies, many of which I participate in occasionally. However, there is one hobby I participate in continuously—writing. Some close to me don't think this is a hobby. This is because I typically write about my profession and sell my books for profit. My books also generate professional speaking engagements, which result in hectic work and travel schedules. It just looks like work to most people.

This leads me to my second point, a point beyond "fish now." Find a way to combine your hobby and your work. I personally hope I am writing and speaking about my profession right up to the point when I drop dead. I'll live longer. Patients proved this point to me just as they proved Dr. Waldridge's advice to be true. The patients who loved their work and enjoyed it like a hobby always seemed to be the happiest and healthiest. They also demonstrated the greatest longevity.

Find a hobby, and if possible make it a profitable one.

CHAPTER 12

Look Forward to Something

> 66 Great works are performed not by
> strength, but by perseverance. 99
>
> ~ *Samuel Johnson*

I practiced chiropractic for almost seventeen years. During that period of time I encountered many patients with fatal conditions. I worked with many of these patients as their health deteriorated and they eventually died. As this occurred over the course of years, I became fascinated by the behavior of several of the patients.

Many of the fatally ill patients displayed an unusual will to live until a specific event occurred. Once the event was over, the patient quickly took a turn for the worse and died. The events were usually the birth of a grand child, a daughter's wedding, someone's graduation, or knowing that loved ones would be secure when death finally came.

I had one patient with Multiple Myeloma who lived years longer than anyone could have predicted. He was working through a list of projects he felt were necessary to complete in order to leave his wife secure. I had several grandmothers and great grandmothers who hung on to see the birth of a grandchild. It was remarkable to watch these patients exert their will to live and equally remarkable to watch how rapidly they deteriorated once they were satisfied with their situation or the event they were looking forward to come to pass.

The power they harnessed to live until a situation existed or an event occurred is in all of us. Unfortunately, most of us only harness this amount of will power in times of great hardship. Evoking this power in everyday life is possible and often necessary. There are things to look forward to now. Find it in yourself to see them through.

Goal setting helps us harness this will power. It gives us something to look forward to. Is there something you are looking forward to? If not, find or plan something. Use it to strengthen your determination. Dig deep now, and it will give you the practice to do it again and again.

Many of the patients described above were those from Chapter 11 who were diagnosed with a fatal disease just after retirement. They may not have gotten to enjoy that long-awaited hobby, but they made the most of every last minute. Make use of your minutes now.

CHAPTER 13

Finish Something

> 66 We shall neither fail nor falter, we shall
> not weaken or tire...
> give us the tools and we will finish the job. 99
>
> ~ *Winston Churchill*

Look around you. There is something you have not finished. I'm not talking about something you started today or this week. I am talking about something that you started weeks, months, or years ago. Maybe it is the genealogy you started. Maybe it is the landscaping or remolding project you started but did not finish. Maybe it is a book you were reading, a photo album you were making, or a book you were writing that is now stuffed in a drawer.

Why do I remind you of these half-finished projects? It is because of the effect they have on you. Typically, just the mention of half-finished projects results in feelings of dread and guilt. This is true even if the finished projects are something you really want to do.

You must finish one or more of these projects to get rid of the dread and guilt associated with them. Finishing an unfinished project achieves a goal, turning dread and guilt into satisfaction and pride.

Another benefit of finishing things is the effect it has on the people in your life. If you have a habit of not finishing what you start, it has a negative effect on others and ultimately their opinion of you. The people around you begin to think of you as all talk and no action, lazy, and unreliable. This is especially true if the projects involve the people around you or are career-related.

Becoming a finisher can reverse these negative thoughts and opinions!

There are a few options for becoming a finisher. Pick the most difficult and time-consuming project and get it over with first. Pick a project that will be completed quickly to give your self a quick burst of enthusiasm. Pick the project of highest priority.

One additional tip: if you are not a finisher, one of the reasons may be your inability to say "No.". If you say "Yes" to everything, you gather more projects than you have the time, energy, and resources to complete. Help with saying "No" is on the way; until then, pick an unfinished project and get started.

William James is credited with saying, *"Nothing is so fatiguing as the eternal hanging on of an uncompleted task."* He is absolutely right! Get started and get energized!

Finishing is a habit you can develop and keep.

CHAPTER 14

Say "No!"

> **"** Giving yourself permission to say "No" is liberating. **"**
>
> ~ *Dr. Jeff Miller*

Do you have trouble saying "No" to people? Do you feel like everyone is dumping his or her responsibilities on you? Is it a problem for you? If it is, then start saying "No!"

I know you are saying this is easy for me to say, and it is. I gave myself permission to say "No." And regardless of what anyone says, you cannot develop the ability to say "No" until you give yourself permission too.

Permission must come from you. You are the one in charge of your life. Asking other people allows them to think they are in charge, and they are not likely to give permission. This is especially true if you will be saying "No" to them.

Giving yourself permission to say "No" is liberating, but it comes with responsibilities. The first responsibility is prioritizing your activities. You must learn to prioritize because you are no longer going to take on everything. You must be selective.

You must also learn to say "No" without offending people. This is done in three steps. First, acknowledge to the person asking how important you feel his request is and why it is important. Second, tell him your schedule simply will not allow you to give adequate attention to such an important matter and you feel the matter deserves someone's complete attention. Third, recommend someone you think would possibly do a good job with his request.

If the person you have trouble saying "No" to is your boss, try this. If your plate is already full and you are given more responsibilities, make a list of your current responsibilities and give it to your boss. Ask him to pick which responsibilities he wants put on hold or dropped in order for you to work on the new responsibilities. If he does not help you prioritize and tells you to complete all the responsibilities, start looking for a new job. This sounds drastic, but in reality you will never be able to get  your work done or do it in a remarkable fashion if you have more work than you have the time, talent, and energy to do. This means promotions are not likely to occur.

Give yourself permission now and get started today.

CHAPTER

15 Give Up Something

> **❝**A man is rich in proportion to the number of things which he can afford to let alone.**❞**
>
> ~ *Henry David Thoreau*

I have described how the inability to say "No" can result in more projects and responsibilities than a person can coordinate. Another factor that often leads to this problem may be the inability to leave things alone.

I have this problem. I hate to be left out. I feel like I must be right in the middle of everything. This is especially true if I am already involved. I want to know every detail. This is a real challenge when it comes to delegating projects and responsibilities. It took me years to learn to delegate effectively.

Giving up things is a hard form of saying "No" as you are saying "No" after you are already involved. This is sometimes a sticky situation. When this occurs I use the same formula I recommend for saying "No." Stress the importance of the activity, and tell them you don't want to let your inability to give your complete attention to the project harm the outcome of the project, and recommend your replacement.

One word of warning: when you bow out of an activity or involvement, do so completely. Do not attempt to direct or criticize the actions of those who replace you. If you get out, get out completely. Meddling later will just leave a bad taste in the mouths of those remaining.

Giving up something does not have to be limited to projects and responsibilities. You can always give up bad habits or unnecessary items. This develops self-discipline and character.

In her book, *Give It Up: My Year of Learning to Live Better with Less*, Mary Carlomagno gave up a single item or activity every month for a year. Among these were television, dining out, and cell phones. This sounds terrible to some but in the author's words, "For me, the biggest lesson of all was not about what I had given up, but what I had gained." I agree. I have frequently gained by letting something else go.

CHAPTER 16 — A Place of Your Very Own

> 66 Children love to be alone because alone is where
> they know themselves, and where they dream. 99
>
> ~ *Roger Rosenblatt*

When I sold my chiropractic practice I knew I would miss my patients and practicing, but it was time to move on and I knew it. What surprised me was the first thing I missed. It was my office—not the building in general but my personal office. I had a really nice personal office. It was my spot. It was where I kept my stuff.

The office was upstairs in the Historic old home I had converted to an office. It was large, nineteen feet by twelve feet. It had a fireplace, plenty of bookshelves and room for my big desk, a sofa, and my drum set. It was great. Unfortunately, when I left practice my house was already full, and my office contents ended up in storage.

I missed my office and my stuff tremendously. My private office was where I did my best thinking and everything was at my fingertips. I think it bothered me so much because I am of the firm belief that every person should have something of his or her very own.

I am also of the firm belief that this is more important to some people than others. Personally I like my space, and this is associated with my personality type.

I was once given a personality test prior to employment. I was able to agree with the findings—both strengths and weaknesses. One of the recommendations to others working with me was, "Stand at least three feet from him." This is because one of the things I value of my very own is my personal space.

The *Personal Trainer Manual* published by the American Council on Exercise quotes a study by E.T. Hall that described twelve feet as a public distance, four to twelve feet as a social distance, and eighteen inches to four feet as a personal space, and less than eighteen inches as an intimate space. Personality type determines the degree of comfort people have with these spaces.

If you are like me, I am betting you have space issues too. I think this also means you feel as I do regarding the need for things that are your very own. This is completely O.K. You are not selfish or mean; it is simply the way you are built. Have your own stuff and have your own space to keep it in. It is O.K!

If the adage "opposites attract" applies to you, then your significant other may not understand your space. This can be a problem. The key to resolving the situation is that both parties understand the other's personality type and compromise. You can have your own space but expect company occasionally, and your mate has to understand there are times you need your space.

CHAPTER 17

Get Some Professional Help

> 66 Your mental attitude gives your entire personality a drawing power that attracts the circumstances, things, and people you think about most. 99
>
> ~ *Unknown*

There are times when our moods, thoughts, and actions are more than we are capable of controlling. This is when professional help may be necessary. The trouble here is getting over the stigma that has long been associated with seeking professional mental healthcare.

Maybe the reason you cannot finish things is because you have attention deficit disorder (ADD). Your response to this may be, "He does not...*look at that pretty bird outside*... what *am I going to fix for dinner... why are stop signs red...?* He's right; I cannot keep my mind on things long enough to finish them."

Maybe you are bipolar and realize you have extreme highs and lows. And you say, "That's it! This book was just what I've been looking for. But it probably won't help me at all."

Maybe you are obsessive compulsive and cannot get started changing your outlook until absolutely everything is perfect or or you turn simple tasks into complex processes. If this is you, then you are saying, "O.K. To get started I'll reread the book. Then I'll read it again and take notes. The notes will then have to be typed and indexed. Color-coding might be a good idea. Then I'll look up all the people he quoted and take notes on their work." You become obsessed with the process and ignore the intended result.

I think you get the idea. Maybe you have already been diagnosed or you may suspect a problem of this nature. Don't let it hold you back.

There is no shame in getting professional help. The shame lies in knowing you have one of these conditions and not doing something about it. The condition moves from being a diagnosis to being an excuse. You are the only one other than the doctor (and maybe insurance carrier) that has to know. Medical help can assist you in leveling your playing field.

CHAPTER 18

Be a Coach, Teacher, Mentor, or Tutor

> 66 To be a teacher in the right sense is to be a learner. I am not a teacher, only a fellow student. 99
>
> ~ *Soren Kierkegaard, Danish Philosopher*

One day in undergraduate college my organic chemistry teacher asked if any of us would be interested in tutoring lower levels of chemistry for nursing and general sciences courses. I paid little attention to his announcement. I was straining to maintain a B-plus average and had plenty to deal with in his course. Helping someone else seemed out of the question, at least until he said, "You don't have to be an A student to tutor. Someone at this level with a B or C average can be a big help to someone struggling at a lower level." This caught my attention and I decided to try it.

I tossed my name into the hat as a tutor and had students right away. I tutored individuals and groups. I had a great time and learned more chemistry tutoring than I ever had through individual study. I realized I was expected to have the answers and studied harder to avoid the embarrassment of not knowing the answers.

Tutoring helped struggling students, increased my knowledge, and I got paid to boot. What a deal! This was an incredible boost to my self-esteem.

I once received a fortune cookie that read, "To teach is to learn twice." I usually don't pay attention to fortune cookies, but this one immediately reminded me of tutoring and it was true.

My organic teacher was right; you don't have to be an A student to tutor. A similar example is one of my childhood sports heroes, Sparky Anderson. Sparky is a member of The Baseball Hall of Fame in Cooperstown, NY as a manager. Sparky is one of the top five managers of all time based on total wins. He won two Manager of the Year awards and three World Series. He was the only manager in baseball history to win the World Series in both the National and American leagues until Tony La Russa led the St Louis Cardinals to victory in the 2006 World Series. These are remarkable accomplishments considering Sparky only played one full year in the major leagues himself. Sparky was not an A player, but he was a great coach. Thankfully, he stuck with baseball and the sport; the players and fans benefited from his teaching skills.

Whether you call it coaching, teaching, mentoring, or tutoring, and whether or not you get paid for it, helping others achieve their goals is a great experience.

There are plenty of opportunities to tutor in most communities. Child and adult literacy programs, English as a second language, and small business associations needing tutors are plentiful. Professional trade organizations in your profession may also sponsor mentoring programs.

Helping just one individual through coaching, teaching, or tutoring is a worthy endeavor and leads to a better outlook in your life.

CHAPTER 19 *Help Someone Who Will Never Know*

> ❝Successful people are always looking for opportunities to help others. Unsuccessful people are always asking, 'What's in it for me?'❞
>
> ~ *Brian Tracy*

There are multitudes of charities these days, and they all need help. Unfortunately, there are too many for one person to help, and I am not sure that everyone helping these days is helping for the right reasons.

I once tracked the requests for donations my business received for one year. The requests outnumbered the days we were open that year. It would be impossible to meet a demand of this magnitude. Ultimately, you must prioritize to contribute. The time and funds should be provided to those organizations closest to your heart.

When your contribution is time, be sure you are there for the right reasons. Too many people these days volunteer for their own benefit and not the benefit of those in need. They do it to boost their resume. Community service looks good on a resume, but service for this reason alone is not true community service.

I am not saying that a person should not get credit for their volunteer work. If a person has given of himself to help others, it should be noted. I am simply saying that the true intentions should be pure.

I think the purest example of a person's intent is seen when he helps others and there is no possible recognition or reward for it while on this earth.

There are many avenues for contributing anonymously. One of my favorites is the angel tree program at Christmas time. This program involves giving to needy children who are anonymous to you and you are anonymous to them.

If you don't want to wait until Christmas, grab a couple of trash bags and pick up trash along a highway. Fill both bags and never tell anyone what you did. If someone you know sees you and pats you on the back, great! If not, this still helps us all and it will get you started. If you enjoy this, keep it up. Otherwise let it springboard you toward another anonymous activity that benefits others.

CHAPTER 20 — Learn Something New

> 66 If a man empties his purse into his head, no man can take it away from him. An investment in knowledge always pays the best interest. 99
>
> ~ *Benjamin Franklin*

One winter I took a correspondence course and became a certified locksmith. I did this because I love to learn something new, and picking locks had always fascinated me. At least I was fascinated with what I thought was lock picking.

I grew up watching detective shows on television where someone was always picking a lock with a small tool or an ordinary paper clip. I wanted to be able to do this so I signed up for the course. To my surprise the first lesson in the course focused on television's portrayal of lock picking. The point of the lesson was that the depiction was unrealistic. It is much easier to break the majority of locks than to pick them. It is also cheaper to break and replace most locks than pick them. By the end of the course I knew this was true.

I was disappointed, but I still enjoyed the course and was impressed with what I learned. I learned a great deal about security systems and home protection. I was happy I did it. Like Franklin said, "…knowledge always pays…"

I love learning something new. The sense of accomplishment that comes with learning is a great feeling. The feeling comes easy when we are very young. As we mature, school systems, parents, and other well-meaning organizations and individuals often destroy our ability to achieve this feeling with negative re-enforcement.

Everyone can learn, especially if it is a topic of interest to him or her. What interests you? Make a list of topics and then select one to study. Buy a book or DVD on the subject. Take a class. Look it up on the Internet. Take lessons. Do something to satisfy your curiosity.

When your efforts result in the satisfaction that comes with learning something new, be proud and celebrate!

As for my lock-picking skills, they are improving. Sometimes I open the lock and sometimes I don't. I can pick older locks. Modern locks are harder to pick. I'll get better with time.

Learn something new!

CHAPTER 21

Drive Time

> 66 If money is your hope for independence you will never
> have it. The only real security that a man will have in this
> world is a reserve of knowledge, experience and ability. 99
>
> ~ *Henry Ford*

Earlier I deviated from classical motivational philosophy by recommending the Jerry Springer show. I am back to traditional philosophy now with an oldie but a goody—listening to motivational and educational information while you drive.

All the great motivational writers and speakers recommend it. That is because it works. Listening to motivational and educational information is easy to do. It has been one of the best ways I have found to work toward a positive outlook on a daily basis.

Books, motivational programs, vocabulary builders, language studies, and much, much more are all on tape/CD these days and readily available. I have dozens of them, and I take advantage of them daily. They are especially great for long drives, waiting in airports, and while flying. I have learned a great deal over the years from these materials—enough I'm sure to equal another college degree.

To get the most out of an audio program, I recommend listening to it at least twice. Listen more than twice if the material is extremely important to you. You must listen more than once as your attention while driving is focused primarily on driving. There will be times what you hear simply doesn't register because your mind is focused on the road. Listening a second time or more will allow you to catch the details missed the first time.

Try this and I'll bet you hear something the second listening that you won't remember from the first listening.

People I have recommended this to often respond by saying, "I can't do that every day." That is O.K. It does not have to be daily. Mix it in with the tape/CD you make to sing along with (Chapter 7), the radio, or silence. Start slow and you will eventually find this addicting.

22 Laughing All the Way

> **"**O'er the fields we go, laughing all the way.**"**
>
> ~ *Jingle Bells, James Pierpoint 1857*

A few years ago another chiropractor and I decided to attend a seminar to obtain our continuing education credits for the year. The seminar was in Columbus, Ohio, which meant a road trip of almost four hours. We were interested in the seminar topic, and we also wanted to have some fun.

I suggested that we stock up on comedy tapes and CDs to listen to them as we traveled. I hoped laughing all the way would be a good stress reliever and set the tone for a good weekend. It was and it did.

This is yet another variation on singing to your favorite music or listening to educational materials as you drive. Obviously I have spent a great deal of time driving. If you do not spend a lot of time driving you can still utilize audio programs. Listen while you exercise, do house work, wash the car, or perform other activities.

Years ago I read the book *Anatomy of an Illness* by Norman Cousins. This is Cousins true story of how he helped treat his own Ankylosing Spondylitis with laughter. Cousins watched hours of old comedy films for therapy. Laughter does make you feel better. Another good reference for this is the movie *Patch Adams*. This is a true story of a doctor that uses humor to help his patients. Everyone should read and watch these.

The saying *"Laughter is the best medicine"* is true. It is true whether you are sick or not. Give it a try.

CHAPTER 23

Take Two Vacations

> 66 Every now and then go away and have a little relaxation. To remain constantly at work will diminish your judgment. Go some distance away, because work will be in perspective and a lack of harmony is more readily seen. 99
>
> ~ *Leonardo DaVinci*

I think everyone should take a minimum of two vacations each year. Each one should last at least a week. I recommend one of the weeks be a vacation full of activity and the other involve as little activity as possible.

Vacations that involve non-stop activities like theme parks, sight seeing, hiking, rafting, exercise, and other activities can be exciting, and are a great change of pace. Activities that differ greatly from your normal activities of daily living take your mind off your troubles and away from your normal thought processes. They can refresh your mind and provide life long memories. Everyone should experience this type of vacation at least once a year.

The only draw back here is this type of vacation often leaves you exhausted and needing a vacation from the vacation.

The less active vacation involves getting away from everybody and everything and doing as close to nothing as humanly possible. Renting a cabin in the woods, visiting a spa, or lying on a beach for a week are good examples. This type of vacation will not only rejuvenate your mind but your body as well. Everyone should experience this type of vacation at least once per year.

A couple of drawbacks to this type of vacation are the inability to let go of your activities and interests and keeping the kids entertained.

You may want to mix the two types of vacations. In this case take two vacations per year that begin with a flurry of activity and end with a few days of total rest and relaxation.

CHAPTER 24 Start

> 66Beginning is half done.99
>
> ~ *Rev. Robert H. Schuller*

It is difficult to use information, plans, and processes without modifying them to your individual needs. This goes back to the different types of intelligences. We all process differently. It seems to be human nature to modify things. The most common example of this is in how students use textbooks. The author thinks he has organized the information in just the right manner, yet students underline, highlight, and write all over the book. They are simply trying to make the information their own.

I do this too. For example, I have used Zig Ziglar's seven-step goal-setting process for years. It is simple and very effective. Zig's audio program *Goals* sums up the entire process in an hour for a very reasonable price, and I recommend it highly. However, despite the program being very effective, I added an eighth step to the process in order to make the process my own.

The step I added was setting a starting date for working on each goal. Zig has a target date for completing each goal but does not recommend a starting date. This surprised me initially because Zig tells a story during his program about delaying the start of his weight-loss goal. He said, "I was so sure I could meet the goal, I didn't bother to get started the first twenty eight days." He discussed this procrastination, but it is not addressed in the steps of the process.

I think the start date is vital if you have a tendency to procrastinate. It is also important in shaming or guilt-tripping yourself into starting work on the goal. Otherwise the shame/guilt does not strike until the completion date closes in. By then it may be too late.

As you read this there is something you have delayed starting that is weighing heavy on your mind. Now is the time to jump in there and get started. Get started and get over the guilt of procrastinating. This will lead to finishing the project and being a finisher as as previously recommended.

I have included a "Goal Setting" worksheet in Appendix B to assist you in setting specific goals with start and completion dates. Make a plan and work the plan!

CHAPTER 25

Stepping Stones

> *Accomplish something every day of your life.*
>
> ~ *Walter Annenberg*

People frequently ask me where I find time to do all that I do. When I tell them how I manage my time they don't seem willing to follow my footsteps. It sounds too much like work. The secret is trying to accomplish something every day and avoid wasting time.

Accomplishing something each day is not really difficult. Sometimes the achievements are very small. The trick is making sure that most of the achievements, no matter how small, are stepping stones toward larger achievements or goals. You don't have to accomplish a major goal every day. In fact, that would be impossible.

I have detailed action plans with steps toward all of my goals, and I keep a separate list of "To Dos." I scan these lists at the beginning of each week and make lists of at least six items to be completed for each day of the coming week. I chip away at my goals each week and get the mundane *to dos* over with. As a result, I am productive.

Having a list each day improves my memory and increases my focus. It also provides a great opportunity at the end of each day to feel accomplished when I check off the items on the list.

What happens when you don't get to everything on the list? (There is no way to prevent this from happening occasionally.) Some days are full of unexpected events and fires to put out. When this occurs, simply move the items on your list to the next day. Recover and keep going.

I have found that I make measurable progress if I accomplish at least six items from my two major lists. It is a simple but effective process. If you are already using a daily list and you don't feel like you are making progress, double-check the items on your list. Make sure the list contains more than just mundane daily chores. The list should always contain at least a few stepping stones toward your major goals.

CHAPTER 26 Dress Yourself Up

> 66 Clothes make the man.
> Naked people have little or no influence on society. 99
>
> ~ *Mark Twain*

A simple step toward happiness is dressing your best. I'm not talking about dressing up for special occasions or events. I'm talking about dressing up for no reason at all. People really do treat you better when you are all dressed up.

In undergraduate college my sociology professor gave several lectures on how people respond to different types of dress, and even the colors people wear. The customary dress for your locality and how you fit into the local style also plays a factor in how people interact with you.

As a doctor I wore a shirt and tie the first ten years of practice. I eventually became sick of this style and changed abruptly to scrubs. There was minimal difference in how my long-time patients reacted to me, but there was a huge difference in how new patients reacted to me in scrubs. It was very different from the way new patients had previously reacted to me in a shirt and tie. The shirt and tie was definitely more authoritative, and the patients listened to me and followed more of my advice.

Another aspect of dress and how it relates to how you feel was always evident in my patient's attire. Rarely did a patient in significant pain dress up to come to the office. The exception here was the person who was not hurting when he got dressed and then hurts himself later in the day. I could always tell when a new patient began to feel better because he would begin to pay more attention to his grooming.

I once taught at a college in Florida. Dress for professors included flowery Hawaiian shirts and slacks. The laid-back look worked there, but it would not be very successful at an ivy league school. When I would wear a tie in Florida, everyone wanted to know what the occasion was. I would always tell whoever asked that I dressed up just for them.

Dressing your best does not mean wearing a tux or an evening gown twenty-four/seven. It simply means dressing as good as the best-dressed person you work or hang out with. If you wear a uniform at work, then yours should be the neatest one. It means setting a standard for your dress in public and sticking to it. It means paying attention to your hair, nails, shaving, make-up, scent, breath, shoes, and accessories.

One standard philosophy and motivational principle for success says, "If you want to have something, act as if it is already true." This carries over to your dress. If you want to be successful, dress like it is already true. If you want to be happy, dress like you are happy. Dressing up is a real pick-me-up.

CHAPTER 27

Put a Limit on It

> 66 Love your enemies just in case your friends
> turn out to be a bunch of bastards. 99
>
> ~ R. A. Dickson

One of the reasons you may be unhappy may come from being let down or disappointed by other people. This is especially true if you have always been there for the people who, when you needed them, let you down. You may have been a friend through thick and thin, rushed to their aid during an emergency, helped them financially, or helped them pick up the pieces when their life fell apart. You did this because you cared and because you honestly felt they would do the same for you. Then, when you needed them they were not there, or even worse, they turn out to be the reason for your trouble.

This is a hard situation to deal with. Disappointment is often worse than anger. It simply hurts more.

The people you choose to associate with and how much of a giver you are influence these situations. This means you must ask yourself, "Am I hanging out with the wrong crowd?" And "Am I giving too much?"

You may be associating with too many people who are takers by nature. Givers are often attracted to takers. They feel like they can save them. This is a one-way street. The giver eventually becomes drained, and the taker moves on to the next giver instead of reciprocating.

The key to avoiding disappointment here is to decide how much you can afford to give in each relationship without expecting anything in return. This is difficult and sounds cold, but it is necessary.

This is another reason to do some of your giving anonymously. The expectation of the other people reciprocating is completely removed along with the chances of being disappointed.

The takers and fair-weather friends in your life are the first people you should begin to say "No" to as discussed earlier.

CHAPTER 28

Do the Worst First

> 66 Do something every day that you don't want to do. This is the golden rule for acquiring the habit of doing your duty without pain. 99
>
> ~ *Mark Twain*

Everyone has things they would rather not do or be associated with. They range from small mundane tasks to very difficult, complicated responsibilities. For me, disliked tasks and responsibilities range from going to the grocery store to telling a patient he has a chronic or terminal disease.

Dreading tasks and responsibilities is a major reason for procrastination. Dread can also cause you to avoid the other people involved. Unfortunately, procrastination and dread only prolong the inevitable and may make the job worse in the long run.

Just get it over with, for Pete's sake! Put the undesirable task at the top of your daily list and tackle it first. Do it first, before moving onto more pleasant items on your list.

I wasted days of playtime as a child because I was a picky eater. I would eat the foods I liked first and save the foods I didn't like until last. I would sit there trying to avoid eating the foods I hated all the while knowing I could not leave the table until I had eaten them. I sat there wasting time. Had I eaten the bad stuff first and got it over with, I would have been able to go play sooner. The wisdom of doing the worst first is not easy for children to see. Adults see the wisdom but often revert to childish ways due to habit and a lack of self-discipline.

Chapter 24 describes the importance of starting. Combining the habit of getting started with doing the worst thing first is a powerful one-two punch for learning the habits to be successful and happy.

Doing the most dreaded task first is a tough habit to develop. It requires great self-discipline. Once developed, however, it is one of the best habits to have. Doing the worst thing first leaves you feeling more accomplished than when you concentrate only on the simple or pleasant tasks. The dread, guilt, and procrastination are all reduced with the principle of doing the worst first.

CHAPTER 29

What's Right?

> 66 Gratitude is born in hearts that take
> time to count up past mercies. 99
>
> ~ *Charles E. Jefferson*

What's wrong? This is a question we have all asked or answered. The funny thing is we never seem to ask or answer the opposite question, "What's right?" The question, "How's it going?" is as close as we typically get.

We all tend to dwell on the negative things in life. This is especially bad for the pessimistic people like me. If I don't immediately think of the negatives, the news media will remind me of them each evening.

What do I recommend here? First, here is a trick I learned from listening to Zig Ziglar. Zig tells two stories about making a list of the positive aspects in your life and another of past accomplishments and positive events.

Zig's first story was about a woman who was extremely negative. He helped her by assisting her in developing a list of positive factors in her life at that time. The second story was of a friend who maintained a list of two hundred positive events and accomplishments from his life.

I suggest we take this advice and make both lists. Make a list of current positive factors in your life; then make a list of the two hundred best things from your life to date. Two hundred sounds like a lot, but you will be surprised how many positives you already have. If you don't have two hundred items to start with, you will remember more later. And you will keep developing the list as life continues.

I titled my life-long list, "Two Hundred Victories/Blessings and Beyond." Blessings on my list include my parents, my wife and children, friends, awards I have won, books and articles I have published, trips I have taken, and many more.

Get busy on those lists.

CHAPTER 30
Mania from the Media

> 66 Reporters thrive on the world's misfortune. For this reason they often take an indecent pleasure in events that dismay the rest of humanity. 99
>
> ~ *Russell Baker*

The news media loves tragedy, war, dirty politics, crime, social unrest, poverty, scandal, and anything else negative. Whatever the situation, the worse it is, the better. The headlines and evening news are full of bad news. Good news is either buried on the back page or limited to a short blurb at the end of the newscast.

The short blurbs at the end of the newscasts are almost amusing. Thirty minutes of depressing information is followed by a short happy segment (usually a human interest story) as though this thirty-second blurb is going to neutralize the preceding thirty minutes of negative information.

I think the overall effect the media has on our lives is negative, and it definitely does not help in the quest for happiness. My recommendation is to reduce your contact with the news media to the smallest amount possible. I am not saying avoid it completely or to the point where you are completely uninformed. However, you definitely should put a limit on the amount of time spent reading and watching bad news.

In addition to negative information, the media is also known for tracking every move of celebrities and other famous people. Personally, I could care less about Brad, Jen, Angelina, Tom, and the rest of the gang. Don't get caught up in this mess. Get busy building your life and stop wasting time reading about and watching other people.

Television has traditionally been the worst of the media addictions. It steals several hours per day from most Americans. This adds up to dozens of hours per week and eventually to hundreds of hours per year. I firmly believe there is a direct correlation between the amount of television watched and the productivity of most people. The more television consumed, the less productive the person. This is now occurring with computers as well.

The Internet is now giving television a run for its money. Surfing the net is becoming as addicting as television. A friend of mine once asked what I did over the weekend. I told him I had written an article and caught up on a few other things. He commented on how productive I was and asked how I found the time to do all I do. I turned the tables and asked him what he did over the weekend. He told me he spent most of the weekend playing a game on the Internet. When pressed, he admitted that the time spent playing the game added up to sixteen hours.

Whether it is the newspaper, tabloid magazines, television, or the Internet, Americans are wasting huge amounts of time on negative unproductive media. Many who read this book and consider the activities suggested will claim they simply do not have the time necessary to perform the tasks. What they are really saying is, "I'm not willing to take time from my unproductive activities and invest it in my happiness." You cannot save time. Time can only be wasted or spent wisely. It is up to you.

CHAPTER 31

Take a Backpack Trip

> 66 He who would travel happily must travel light. 99
>
> ~ *St. Exupery*

The recommended activity in this chapter is fun. I want you to take a trip. You can go anywhere you want, any distance you want, spend as much money as you want, and stay as long as you want. The catch is, you have to pack like a cowboy. Let me explain.

As a child I was fascinated with Indians and cowboys. I grew up with John Wayne movies and television westerns like Gun Smoke and Bonanza. One of the things that fascinated me was the cowboy's ability to roam the west with everything he owned on his horse. Can you imagine, everything we own these days fitting on a horse or even in our cars? Not a chance!

We cannot travel anywhere these days without taking tons of stuff with us. Our cars are full, our suitcases are bulging, and we pack the overhead bin space on airplanes. Nine times out of ten, we don't wear or use half the stuff we drag from place to place. And we buy more stuff wherever we go.

My suggestion is to take a trip that is all about the experience and not about stuff. Do not take more stuff than will fit in a backpack or its equivalent. Don't take more than you can carry on your back. You will avoid packing the car, checking baggage, lost baggage, bellhops, and the stress of keeping up with all your stuff. You can focus on your activities and/or rest.

Obviously, it is difficult to take the kids along on these trips. This is especially true if they are small. Strollers, car seats, diaper bags, extra clothes, food, and toys are the norm here. Take this trip with your spouse, friend, or by yourself.

There are so many things that can go wrong while traveling with tons of stuff. Traveling light reduces the negative possibilities and makes traveling more fun. Try it even if it is just for a weekend. I think you will be surprised at how liberating and fun it can be.

CHAPTER 32 *Act on an Idea*

> 66 An idea not coupled with action will never get any
> bigger than the brain cell it occupied. 99
>
> ~ *Arnold Glasow*
>
> 66 If I have a thousand ideas and only one turns out to
> be good, I am satisfied. 99
>
> ~ *Alfred Nobel*

Everyone has ideas. Sometimes they are good and sometimes they aren't so good. Mostly they aren't so good. Since most aren't so good, many of us get discouraged after a few ideas fail and start ignoring our ideas.

Don't fall into this mindset. If your ideas have not been working out, don't quit; just move onto the next idea. Think about the quote above by Alfred Nobel. Nobel was a very accomplished man. If he can be satisfied with one good idea out of a thousand, we should be.

A similar quote by Thomas Edison comes to mind. "I have not failed. I've just found ten thousand ways that won't work." This statement was made by Edison after over ten thousand attempts to develop the light bulb. Most of us would not have tried one hundred times much less ten thousand times.

It is one thing to carry through with an idea and have it fail. It is another thing altogether to give up on an idea before following through. Giving up half way through and never knowing if the idea was good or bad can be regretful. This is especially true if an idea is abandoned and someone else comes along and succeeds with the same idea.

Don't give up on your ideas. Write them down; then act on them. Some of them will work and some of them will not. Remember, in order to have a really great idea you have to have a lot of ideas. Try them all.

Do you have an idea for a product, process, craft, business, hobby, game, service, etc? Have you delayed taking action on an idea that may be the big one? Well get busy and give it a try. If it flops, then dust yourself off and start on the next idea.

CHAPTER 33

Honor Someone

> 66 It is said that a man to whom a book is dedicated always buys a copy. If this is true in this instance, a princely affluence is about to descend on the author. 99
>
> *~ Mark Twain*

The quote above is from the dedication of Twain's book, *The Celebrated Jumping Frog of Calaveras County and Other Sketches.* The book was dedicated to John Smith. In his wit and wisdom, Twain, knowing John Smith was a common name, hoped all of the gentlemen with the name would think the book was dedicated to them and would buy a copy.

As a humorist Mark Twain made a joke of his dedication. True dedications are meant to honor people. This book is dedicated to my sister. I have dedicated previous books to my wife and children and my mother. This is one of my favorite parts of writing. I enjoy honoring those I love and I hope they feel honored. I hope it is a very special feeling.

Are there people in your life that you would like to honor? Is there a parent, sibling, friend, co-worker, teacher, etc. that has been a large influence in your life? If so, find a way to honor them. Dedicate a book to them, make a contribution to a church or charity in their name, throw a party for them, name something or someone after them, or build something in their honor. My best friend Dan named the puppy we gave him "Miller" after me. I was flattered. He grew up to be a good dog.

I have had the opportunity to know and work with doctors all over the country. One of the things I used to do when I was impressed with another doctor and wanted to show my appreciation was to write a letter to the editor of the newspaper in his/her town.

The letters told how I came to know the doctor, listed his accomplishments, explained why the doctor impressed me, and stated why the community should feel lucky to have the doctor. Most of the letters I wrote were published. A few were not. When one of the letters made it into print, the doctor was usually surprised and flattered. The letters were always great public relations for the doctors.

I have read that one of the top rewards people seek for their work is appreciation. Appreciation is said to be ahead of money on the list of occupational rewards. Everyone wants to be appreciated at work and in all other aspects of life. Honoring someone makes them feel appreciated, and in the long run both parties are happy.

My friend Dan once asked me how I got my name in the paper so frequently. I told him I had a good PR person (me). He said, "I would have to kill someone to get in the paper." He was just kidding. When he did get his name in the paper I went down to the local sporting goods store and bought him a trophy. It was a big trophy with a fish on top. I called it "The Big Fish in the Small Pond Award." The engraving at the bottom of the trophy read, "You Da Man."

He gave it back to me later in recognition of one of my accomplishments. This led to us passing the trophy back and forth and to other friends each time that recognition was due. It has been a great way to honor each other and our friendships. It has also been great fun and a good conversation piece for years.

Recognize someone you appreciate!

CHAPTER 34

Keep Busy

> **66** I never remember feeling tired by work, though idleness exhausts me completely. **99**
>
> ~ *Sherlock Holmes*

One of the best tricks I have learned for staying positive is to stay busy. Not busy to the point where I had no free time, but busy enough to keep my mind off my troubles.

Too much free time on your hands just leads to trouble. There is too much time to sit and worry about your trouble, imagining the worst and become overly conscious of every little ache and pain. It can be depressing. Don't fall into this trap.

Most of the recommended activities in this book will take one to two weeks to carry out. Mixed in with your daily responsibilities at work and home, they should be enough to keep you busy and avoid the ills of idleness.

This is the theme of the entire book—action. There are multitudes of books and seminars that give pep talks. Positive words are great, but positive actions are much better. It has been said, "You are what you **think** about all day long" and "In order to be (have or do) something, you must **act** as if it is already true." **Thinking** about something is one thing. **Acting** on an idea is another. Action is more powerful. To quote another old saying, "Action speaks louder than words."

35 Give Great Gifts

> 66It is not the weight of jewel or plate, or the fondle of silk or fur; Tis the spirit in which the gift is rich, As the gifts of the Wise Ones were, And we are not told whose gift was gold, Or whose was the gift of myrrh.99
>
> ~ *Edmund Vance Cooke*

Both of my parents grew up very poor in families with eleven or more children. The bare necessities were hard to come by, and they had to work from the time they were very young. Special occasions like Christmas and birthdays were tough for them as there was little if any money for celebrations and gifts.

Both of my parents developed very strong work ethics as a result of their upbringing. However, their outlooks on Christmas, birthdays, and gift giving were very different. My mother has always made Christmas and birthdays very special celebrations putting great effort into each event. My mother especially loves Christmas, and she always wanted my sister and me to have what she missed as a child.

My father was just the opposite. He never really experienced Christmas or other holidays as a child, and as a result he never seemed to think they were important. He made an effort for his children, but you could tell he was seldom in the holiday spirit. He was a terrible gift giver. He had my mother's help when it came to the kids, but he was terrible when it came to buying gifts for her. He waited until the last minute and put little if any thought into selecting gifts for her.

My mother's disappointment in his gifts was often very obvious. This had a profound effect on me. I promised myself I would be a good gift giver when I grew up. Eventually, my sister began dragging my father and his checkbook out to shop each year at Christmas. This made a big difference in his gift-giving abilities.

Being a good gift giver takes a lot of effort. It requires paying attention to other people's interests, desires, hobbies, and dreams. It requires thought and effort. Pay attention to things they say about items, especially the ones they look at but won't buy for themselves. Money helps but it is not the primary factor. It is more important for a gift to be appropriate, needed, desired, or meaningful than it is for the gift to be expensive.

Being a good gift giver is a challenge but one worthy of meeting. Meeting the challenge means bringing joy and happiness to those you love, and in turn you will bring happiness to yourself. Pay attention to the interests, desires, hobbies, and dreams of those you love and use this information when selecting gifts for them.

CHAPTER 36 — Make Your Own Luck

> 66 God doesn't play Dice. 99
>
> ~ *Albert Einstein*

The quote above is true, and since God doesn't play dice you shouldn't play dice either. I'm speaking literally and figuratively. You should not play dice or other games of chance where betting is involved. Don't throw away your hard-earned money.

Television these days frequently broadcasts poker tournaments. Casinos and bingo parlors are popping up everywhere. The lottery is going strong in almost every state. Gambling occurs on the Internet and in the stock market.

The poker craze is the most disturbing to me. I have already met two young men fresh from high school who are convinced that they are going to make their fortunes playing poker. They have given up on higher education, learning a trade, or getting a steady job. Both have already brought great grief and financial problems to their parents. Neither of these young men seems conscious of their true situation, and both are quick to claim their salvation is in the next hand of cards.

These young men would never think they could make it big in the National Basketball Association (NBA). They are both short and uncoordinated. They think their big break lies in poker because poker provides the illusion that anyone can win big because anyone can play.

While there is some degree of skill in card playing, the overwhelming factor in the outcome of the game is chance.

Don't leave your life to chance. Plan your life and work your plan. No action is action. No decision is a decision. Make the overwhelming factor in your life planning and goal setting.

I recommend the goal-setting program offered in Zig Ziglar's audio program *Goals*. The program has seven steps for planning every goal: listing the goal, describing why you want to achieve the goal, setting a date for completion, listing the skills and resources needed to achieve the goal, listing the people and organizations you need to associate with in order to achieve the goal, listing obstacles that will have to be overcome in order to achieve the goal, and listing the action steps necessary for achieving the goal. (See Appendix B.)

As I mentioned earlier I add an additional step to goal setting. I have found that setting a starting date is as important as setting a completion date. All of this information must be written down. Putting the goal and its parameters on paper strengthens the goal in your mind and is the first step toward completion. I once read in a business manual that a scheduled activity is eight hundred times more likely to occur than an unscheduled activity. Even if this was an exaggeration and a scheduled activity is only ten times more likely to occur, you should write everything down.

37 You Are Never Too Old

> 66And in the end, it's not the years in your life that count. It's the life in your years.99
>
> ~ *Abraham Lincoln*

> 66Anyone who stops learning is old, whether this happens at twenty or eighty. Anyone who keeps on learning not only remains young, but becomes constantly more valuable regardless of physical capacity.99
>
> ~ *Harvey Ullman*

In the early 1990's I was studying for my orthopedic specialty. During this time I became friends with another chiropractor named Charlie. We attended the seminars and training sessions together for over three years. Charlie had entered the program before I did and had the opportunity to take the boards a year before I was eligible. Charlie failed his first attempt by just a few points.

By the next year I was eligible for the boards, and Charlie and I spent a great deal of time studying together. We lived over one hundred miles apart but traveled back and forth on weekends to study and plan our trip to Dallas for part one of the board examination.

Charlie and I were successful in Dallas and again in Los Angeles for part two. We obtained our orthopedic specialties. It felt great to pass, especially with a good friend.

Charlie and I were an odd couple. I was in my late twenties and Charlie was in his early sixties. He was older than my father, but we got along like two kids. This was because Charlie was a good-natured big-hearted guy who was always quick to smile. He loved our profession and the people in it. Charlie was sixty-five years old when we passed our boards. He taught me that no one is ever too old to learn or achieve.

In recent years I have suffered through a terrible period of illness and a career crisis. I fell into a rut of thinking I was a tired sick old man at forty-three. Thinking of Charlie and his will to live, learn, and help when he was well past the age of forty-three helps me move forward and look beyond my trouble.

Charlie passed away in his seventies. He passed away in his office working at what he loved and was loved for. God bless the *Charlies* in our lives.

You are never too old!

38 Reward Yourself

> 66 The rewards for those who persevere far exceed the pain that must precede the victory. 99
>
> ~ *Ted W. Engstrom*

When you accomplish the projects recommended in this book you will be rewarded. Your reward will be happiness, being more self confident, and having more self-esteem. In addition to these rewards I recommend you give yourself another reward when you have completed several of the projects described.

I recommend you reward yourself after you have completed at least half of the projects in this book. I recommend a second reward when you finish all the projects in the book. If you do not want to wait this long for the first reward, you can give it to yourself sooner. You may need the encouragement. I would not recommend waiting longer than the halfway point in order to avoid being discouraged.

The reward must have clear parameters. The finish line must be crossed before you reward yourself. You absolutely must not give yourself the reward before you have reached the established target.

The reward can be very simple and inexpensive or very elaborate and expensive. It can be a trip, concert, book, clothes, jewelry, furniture, vehicles, or what ever you wish. You should select the reward before becoming fully

involved in the projects. It should be something you would not buy out of necessity. The reward should be something you will keep for a long period of time or will provide a long-term happy memory. It can be something just for you or something that you share with others. The reward cannot be something you have to go into debt for. The reward should not have any negative aspects.

The purpose here is to reward yourself for a job well done. This is positive reinforcement. The reward is an opportunity to stop and smell the roses that bloom as a result of your hard work.

CHAPTER 39 Do Something Goofy/Adventurous

> 66 Not one shred of evidence exists in favor of the idea
> that life is serious. 99
>
> ~ *Brendan Gill*

I spent over a decade testifying in chiropractic malpractice cases as an expert witness. During that time I became friends with one of the attorneys I worked with, Steve. Steve is a great guy and I have always enjoyed our friendship. Steve is in a serious and sometimes very negative business, but he doesn't let it spill over into his personal life.

Frequently when I hear from Steve, he is on his way to or from some event. Riding his motorcycle, Jimmy Buffet concerts, and trips to Florida are typical.

Once he told me he had just returned from a big pro-wrestling event. While I was used to hearing of his escapades, the wrestling event surprised me. When I asked him what the attraction was, he told me it was "mindless fun." He said he could cheer and jeer, let off some steam, and just have fun doing something completely different. Pro-wrestling is definitely different.

Something completely different and kind of crazy is good occasionally. It distracts your mind from your troubles, gets you out of a rut, and it is fun and refreshing. It can be anything you want it to be. Just remember to ask yourself two questions when you come up with something goofy to do. Is it different? Is it fun?

I have in recent years made a habit of doing something goofy or adventurous for my birthday. Hiking in the mountains, a hot air balloon ride, white-water rafting, and tubing down a lazy river have been among the most recent activities. I have a list I am working through. Parasailing, a monster-truck rally, deep-sea fishing and others are coming up.

What are you going to do?

40 *Know the Score*

> 66 We're not completely happy here because we're not supposed to be! Earth is not our final home; we were created for something much better. 99
>
> ~ *Rick Warren*

A friend of mine is an avid NASCAR fan. He follows everyone and everything in the sport. He hates to miss a race. Luckily with today's advances in electronics, he does not have to miss a race. The recording device connected to his satellite television allows him to record any race and watch it later.

One weekend his work conflicted with the racing schedule so he set the recorder and went to work. On his way home he stopped for gas. While in line to pay he overheard the two men in front of him talking about the race. Their conversation revealed the highlights and result of the race. He was disappointed but returned home to watch the race anyway. He is a true fan.

When he told me how discovering the outcome of the race disappointed him, he made note of another interesting fact about this occurrence. Typically when he watches a race, live or recorded without knowledge of the outcome, he says he feels apprehensive. He is on the edge of his seat with every lead change, accident, caution flag, etc. This continues until his favorite driver is either out of the race or the race is over. I know how he feels. I am not a race fan, but I am a big University of Kentucky basketball fan. I'm on the edge of my seat when UK plays, especially during close games.

He said knowing the outcome ahead of time prevented his normal apprehension. He was able to watch the game very calmly.

I think there is a lesson here. I think the calm he felt is similar to the calm felt by Christians as they travel through life. They know the final outcome and are able to watch the race of life with less apprehension and worry.

I say "less" because it is human nature to worry and be apprehensive. Once we acknowledge the final outcome, we must constantly redirect our attention to it as we go.

Do you know the final outcome?

41

Exercise or Rot

> 66 Iron which is not whetted will grow rusty;
> water which does not flow will become stagnant. 99
>
> ~ *Chinese Proverb*

There, I said it. You knew it was coming. You have to exercise. Remember the eustress discussed earlier? Have you done anything about it yet? Well, the time is now.

I recommend you hire a personal trainer and/or join a gym that has trainers. I say this because the average person really doesn't know enough about exercise to set goals, get started, and do it safely. I know they don't know because even as a doctor I didn't know much about exercise.

Hundreds of topics are covered in a health-care education. Unfortunately, there are so many, exercise receives little attention. Exercise is covered but not to the degree so that most health-care providers can do a *good* job of prescribing it. A doctor can and should tell you if you are capable of exercising. However, unless a doctor has taken additional training in exercise prescription, he cannot typically make more than vague non-specific recommendations about how to exercise.

My father died at an early age. He was diabetic, smoked heavily, and never exercised. After his death I decided to get in shape in order to live longer. To do this I knew in spite of my health-care training I had to learn more about exercise. I then sought out and completed certifications in strength conditioning and personal training.

I can say with confidence that increased knowledge about why and how to exercise made all the difference in starting and maintaining an effective exercise program.

Some need the attention of a trainer one-on-one for a prolonged period, and others can get started with a trainer and then exercise alone. If you carry on alone it is a good idea to have the trainer check your progress occasionally.

A well-rounded exercise program addresses flexibility, strength, and aerobic conditioning. When the factors are all present, exercise will help reduce weight, control weight, reduce stress (distress), improve strength, increase flexibility, condition the heart and lungs, build bone density, and dozens of other positive benefits (eustress).

If you are wondering which exercise is the best, consider the following; Walking is the easiest, cheapest, and most beneficial to start and continue. Finally, the best overall exercise in my clinical and personal experience is… the exercise you will do!

CHAPTER 42 Study Your Heroes

> **66** I am not a role model. **99**
>
> ~ *Charles Barkley*

My biggest childhood hero was Johnny Bench, the Hall of Fame catcher for the Cincinnati Reds. I loved watching him play and learning about him. I have also had heroes as an adult. Yes, adults can have heroes. Motivational writer, speaker, and coach Steve Chandler who wrote the foreword to this book is one of my heroes.

We should have heroes throughout life. Having heroes helps us strive to do better. It helps us understand that ordinary people can achieve great things. Yes, I said ordinary people. All heroes are basically ordinary people who have managed to do extraordinary things. In fact, most heroes are only extraordinary in one area of their lives. Remember the different types of intelligences described in Chapter 2?

Several years ago the public was outraged when NBA basketball player Charles Barkley said he wasn't a role model and didn't want to be one. He was criticized heavily for this comment. After all, he was famous; and the youth of America looked up to Charles. He should be a role model. I was shocked at first; then I realized he was just being honest. Just because he can play basketball, it does not mean he does everything well or that he is perfect.

Barkley was being honest and in doing so took the monkey off his back when it comes to the rest of his life. Famous people often have their personal and professional lives placed under a microscope and extreme scrutiny. Denying the role-model status removed the shock value the press would have if he did or said something controversial. If something controversial comes up, his response will naturally be, "I told you I'm not a role model."

Barkley is smart. So many athletes, actors, musicians, politicians, ministers, and others with wide media coverage and fame have been portrayed as perfect role models only to fall from grace because of gambling, alcohol, drugs, sex, influence pedaling, and many other problems. Scandal can happen to any "ordinary" person, hero or not.

I again refer to heroes as ordinary because they are just that—ordinary people. They are ordinary people who have been able to focus on their strongest type of intelligence and thus accomplish something great. Barkley, like the rest of us, has different combinations of the seven major intelligences. He used his bodily-kinesthetic intelligence to achieve in basketball.

Like intelligences, personality types are another factor that reminds us that heroes are just ordinary people. Many people famous for extraordinary use of one of their intelligences have personality quirks. Actions related to personality type and how they affect judgment in personal relationships help create some of the problems that lead to the scandals mentioned above.

Study heroes. But remember they will all have faults and personality quirks. Some of them will be bigger heroes and role models than others. None of them are or were perfect. Take from your study the idea that you too can focus your stronger intelligences toward great achievements. You can be a hero in someone's life.

Read a book or watch a documentary about one of your heroes.

43 Do Something for a Child

> 66 To ease another's heartache is to forget one's own. 99
>
> ~ *Abraham Lincoln*

My wife Kim teaches three- and four-year-old pre-schoolers with special needs. They have Down's syndrome, Cerebral Palsy, Autism, and other conditions. Some are children of drug addicts and alcoholics. Some have been physically and/or sexually abused. Some speak little or no English. Some are still not potty trained.

Kim has forty students daily, twenty in the morning for three hours and twenty in the afternoon for three hours. Kim, her assistants, and an army of speech therapists, social workers, and other specialists face a wide variety of challenges every day. The efforts that go into simple things like learning colors or climbing the stairs on the bus are remarkable.

I visit her classroom occasionally, and the children are sweet. Unfortunately, I cannot handle being there long. I feel so bad for these children and it upsets me. Unlike my wife and her associates, I am just not cut out for this environment. I don't possess the patience, skill, and love required to address the needs of these children.

Outside of my own children, I am not comfortable with children for more than a few minutes. I am much more comfortable with adults and their needs. When I practiced, the vast majority of my patients were between the ages of eighteen and fifty-five years of age.

Even though I am not a child-oriented person, I still like doing something for children. It is very rewarding.

Providing for child's nourishment, safety, education, or health can be done through a variety of methods. Financial support, church missions, Sunday schools, reading programs, baby sitting, food and clothing donations, and angel trees are just a few.

One of the ways I used to contribute to children in the community where I practiced was collecting food donations from patients in exchange for a day's care once every six months. The food bank in town told me that donations of canned goods (beets, spinach, and other foods children typically dislike) are little help for hungry children. Peanut butter and crackers and macaroni and cheese were said to be the most beneficial. On the donation days, I worked all day for donations of peanut butter, crackers, and macaroni and cheese.

Doing this twice a year helped in another way. Everyone is always acutely aware of donating at Thanksgiving and Christmas. Donations are much less abundant during the remainder of the year. I held the first donation day at holiday time. I held the second donation day in late spring just before school was out. This helped the children who would go through the summer without free school lunches.

Please help a child. You will help yourself just as much.

CHAPTER 44
Do Something for the Elderly

> 66 We can do no great things, only small things with great love. 99
>
> ~ *Mother Teresa*

My mother is a nurse who spent most of her career working in nursing homes. She worked the 3 p.m. to 11 p.m. shift most days, and I would often stop to see her on my way home from school. When I visited she would always introduce me to her co-workers and patients.

One gentleman she introduced me to (I think his name was Mr. Harris) was a life-time bachelor who had no family or friends left to visit him. He had been a reporter and editor for a small-town Kentucky newspaper. When we met he immediately began to show me clippings of old articles he had written years before and wanted to tell me every detail of each story. He had piles of these old yellowed clippings.

I began to stop by each time I visited my mother and talk with him for a few minutes. Each time we relived one or two of his stories from the clippings. It seemed to make him happy, and I enjoyed it too. I cannot say for sure, but he may have had some influence on my desire to write. I eventually lost touch with him when I left for college, and I think he died a short time after.

My father spent his last days in one of the nursing homes my mother had worked in. I used to go see him after work just to talk as I had with the other gentleman. My father was not coherent enough to talk much, and by that time he thought I was his brother Bob. At least it was Bob one day and the next day his brother Tom. I often wished he had been coherent enough to talk like Mr. Harris had with me years before.

One day as I was leaving after visiting my father, a small frail little lady came shuffling down the hall toward me. She stopped just before we were close together and started staring down at her shoes. When I reached her she lifted her head and said sadly, "My shoe is untied." I looked down and she was wearing a small pair of plaid sneakers; the left laces were untied.

"I'll tie your shoe," I said. "You probably tied mine plenty of times." It was my first-grade teacher. I had heard she was in the home suffering from Alzheimer's disease. I kneeled down and tied her shoe and checked the other one while I was at it. When I stood she reached up and put her hand on my right cheek and said, "You're little Kenneth Jeffrey aren't you?" I said, "Yes I am." It had been almost thirty years since she taught me, and I had only seen her a few times in between first grade and that moment. Despite the Alzheimer's she knew me.

Remarkable! She smiled again, patted me on the arm and began shuffling off down the hall again.

When my wife Kim and I were selecting names for our first daughter, we agreed that we had never met an Emily that we did not like and we liked the name. My first grade teacher was one of those Emilys, and one of the ones our Emily is named for.

Tying her shoe was a simple thing but as the quote above says, "We can do no great things, only simple things with love." I was just returning one of the many small favors she had given to me. This is something we can all do.

CHAPTER 45 Identify Your Triggers

> 66 Real valor consists not in being insensible to danger, but in being prompt to confront and disarm it. 99
>
> ~ *Sir Walter Scott*

If you have tendencies to be depressed and have pessimistic moods brought on by situations and thoughts that can be identified, you can learn to recognize and control these situations and thoughts. They are often called triggers.

Triggers are the events and situations that cause a mood swing from one mood to the next. Learning to recognize and control triggers are keys to living life without drastic mood swings.

Recognizing a trigger begins with paying attention to the situations and events that are present when you are up and when you are down. In other words, notice what makes you happy and what makes you sad. Pay attention to what lifts your spirits, what makes you smile, and what makes you feel confident. Likewise, pay attention to what makes you anxious, what worries you, and what you fear.

Once triggers are identified, the mission is to avoid the negative ones and try to use the positive ones to help control mood swings.

Some triggers are small, and several may have to build over time in order to trigger a mood swing. Others are more significant and can trigger mood swings rather quickly. In some situations you may have to identify several small triggers or a few more significant triggers to get a handle on your situation and improve your mood.

In addition to events and situation, triggers can also be people. Some people can completely drain and depress you. Others lift your spirits, inspire you, and make you smile. If someone is bad for you, you may simply need to avoid him at all cost. If someone motivates you, then you should keep him around.

46 *Upside Down from the End Backwards*

> 66 Conquering any difficulty always gives one a secret joy, for it means pushing back a boundary-line and adding to one's liberty. 99
>
> ~ *Henri Frederic Amiel*

I began my college career as a music major (percussionist) at Eastern Kentucky University. It was a great deal of fun. I met several of the most interesting people I have ever known. One of these individuals was the professor of percussion, Dr. Donald Cooper.

Dr. Cooper was probably the coolest person I have ever known. When he walked into a room, everyone took notice. He had a striking appearance. He wore dark suits, was always tan, and his hair and goatee were silver. Everything he did was smooth: walk, talk, play the drums, and even smoke. It was the eighties, but if it had been the sixties he would have been described as "Cool, Man, Cool."

Dr. Cooper had played with some of the biggest names in the music business. He once took me to a Percussive Arts Society convention in Indianapolis, and many of the most famous drummers in the world came over and said, "Hey Don, how've ya been?" I spent the weekend with him and many of my other heroes. At the age of eighteen that's a "Wow"!

In addition to music Dr. Cooper loved to fly his plane and play golf. In fact he passed away doing one of the things he loved. He suffered a heart attack in the middle of a round of golf.

As my teacher for private lessons, he liked to have me play music sight unseen or sustain a drum roll while he recorded it on an old reel-to-reel tape machine. He always played the recording back at a really slow speed. No matter how well I thought the music or the roll sounded at normal speed, it sounded terrible slowed down to the individual stroke. The goal was to make every stroke sound the same.

The challenges were fun during the lessons, but less fun in real-life situations. Dr. Cooper provided one of those real-life situations for me during my second music jury. A jury was a panel of three music professors: the one who taught your private lessons and two others. To receive your final grade for the lesson class, you had to perform for the panel. The professors critiqued your performance and could ask questions about the music of that performance or anything else you had played during the semester.

I played a four-mallet marimba arrangement and a snare drum piece. During the snare drum piece, the three professors left their positions behind the table and stood behind me. They watched the music and listened as I played. It went well and I was glad it was over. At least I thought it was over.

The panel commended my performance and then Dr. Cooper said, "Now comes the fun part." He took the music off the stand, turned it upside down, and said, "Now play it upside down from the end backwards."

I am sure I looked at him as though he was kidding. The other professors began to laugh, but Cooper was serious. I knew from his sadistic grin he was not kidding. I looked at the music and realized I had to reverse all of the rhythms; I took a deep breath and started playing. I played the first line without missing a note. He then stopped me and told me I passed the test.

At first I didn't know if I should be upset about the curve he threw me or to be pleased with myself. Later I was pretty happy.

It may seem like a minor challenge in life, but I have thought about that day frequently over the years. I have thought about the stress of the situation, pulling the rabbit out of the hat, and the confidence Dr. Cooper had in me to do what he asked. He helped me have confidence in myself. It was a wonderful lesson from a wonderful teacher. I miss him.

Be on the lookout for things you can do in a completely different way than you have ever done them before. Challenge yourself to solve a problem by working from the end backwards.

CHAPTER 47 *Make Peace with Your Regrets*

> 66 Regret for things we did can be tempered by time; it is regret for the things we did not do that is inconsolable. 99
>
> ~ *Sidney Smith, English Clergyman*

We all have regrets in life, and we have them in varying degrees. A few of us have the attitude toward regrets that is expressed in the song *MacAuthor Park*, "Regrets, I've had a few, but then again, too few to mention." Others of us have many regrets and have a difficult time letting them go.

I don't think it is possible to let regrets go completely. As the quote above relates, they can be tempered at best.

My paternal grandparents died long before I was born, as did my maternal grandfather. Thus, I only knew my maternal grandmother and her second husband as grandparents. They were very sweet people and I loved them. Unfortunately, I only saw them once a year, and they were always in poor health. Very little of my time with them was spent doing many of the things grandparents and grandchildren usually do.

The few memories I do have of spending time with them are mainly of time with my grandfather. His name was John and all of the grandchildren called him Papaw. He was a big man, a World War I veteran, and a carpenter most of his life. He was missing the ring finger on one hand. The missing finger wasn't from the war but from an accident with dynamite. He had been trying to remove tree stumps from a farm he lived on.

Papaw smoked a pipe and cigars and chewed tobacco. Sometimes he did more than one of these at the same time. He always gave me a cigar with a plastic tip so I could imitate him, and he taught me how to spit. When I was with him I ran around with the cigar in my mouth, taking it out only to spit, and I had a big ring of Kool-Aid around my mouth. This was a sight that once proved embarrassing for my mother when he was babysitting me. She asked him to bring me to the hospital my grandmother was in to meet some of her old nursing friends. They met a cigar smoking, spitting, Kool-Aid-stained five-year-old.

I am not sure if it was his advancing age or a long-standing lack of skill, but he was a terrible driver. He drove on the curbs, in the middle of the road, in other lanes, and yes, occasionally on the sidewalk—all at breakneck speeds. It was great fun for a five-year-old. When I was little I thought he drove like that to amuse me. As I got older I realized that was just the way he actually drove. There were no car seats then. I was standing in the front seat next to him.

My grandmother passed before my grandfather, and he was left alone in poor health. At age fourteen I visited him for what I did not know would be the last time. He wanted me to stay with him, but at fourteen, I wanted to spend the time with my cousins. I was a typical teenager and wanted to hang out and have fun.

A month later I was at band camp far from home, and my parents and sister showed up unexpectedly. I knew something terrible had to be wrong, and it was. Papaw had passed away. I was very hurt, and all I could think about was missing my last chance to spend time with him because of my own selfishness.

I have carried that regret well into adulthood. It still bothers me.

I have other regrets for my actions and inactions in life. In fact I recently made a list of them. I am working through forgiving myself and trying to correct, if possible, any harm I've done. I doubt this will ever resolve the regrets, but at least it will help temper them.

Make your list, make your peace, and continue.

48 *Collect Experiences*

> 66 Life isn't a matter of milestones, but of moments. 99
>
> *~ Rose Kennedy*

I have moved several times in the last few years. The good news is that it has been the result of positive career moves and up-grading homes. The bad news is that moving is always a pain, regardless of the reason.

An additional bit of good news rests in the opportunity moving provides for assessing what you own. You can sort through all your stuff. Doing this may bring back some of the favorite memories discussed earlier. It will also afford you the chance to get rid of stuff that you no longer want or need. Moving can then be a cleansing experience.

After moving my stuff several times in recent years, I have decided I have more than I need. This has led to my decision to stop collecting stuff and focus more on collecting experiences.

For so many, including myself, the American dream has been steeped in the accumulation of material items. While it is good to have nice things, there is a point where you transition from owning items to the items owning you.

To avoid this I have been slowly weeding out unwanted and unneeded items. I have also begun scrutinizing my purchases more carefully. When it comes to gifts I have asked those who buy gifts for me to consider buying tickets to events, certificates to restaurants, memberships to museums/theaters, and other things that do not take up space, and/or require upkeep. I request these gifts be good for two or more people so I can share the moments.

I have decided to collect moments instead of stuff from now on. I want to collect moments from time spent with family, friends, co-workers, and even perfect strangers. Yes, even perfect strangers.

Recently, I had two layovers in the Charlotte, North Carolina airport. Charlotte has rocking chairs in several locations throughout the terminal. They are large wooden chairs painted white. They are comfortable and popular, and it is sometimes difficult to get one if the airport is busy. I was lucky to get a rocker during each layover. I was also lucky enough to sit next to someone I could strike up a conversation with.

The first person was a fellow from New Jersey and the second was a lady from Pennsylvania. They were two of the nicest conversations I have had in a long time. We talked about a wide variety of topics. They were very pleasant moments.

Moments occur in two ways. Some are unexpected and others are planned. Either way we want them all to be "Good Moments."

Learn to cherish moments and experiences. Stop worrying about your stuff, whether it be that you have too much of it or not enough of it.

49 Help Others by Helping Yourself

> 66It is one of the most beautiful compensations of life that no man can sincerely try to help another without helping himself.99
>
> ~ *Ralph Waldo Emerson*

Everyone who suffers from being down in the dumps, depression, or whatever it's called, has to realize that you are seldom there alone. You are there with your family, friends, co-workers, and other people you come in contact with. They may not be pessimistic or depressed, but your pessimism and depression certainly affect them.

Depressed feelings are accompanied by decreased self-esteem and self-pity. We become self-absorbed and so focused on our own problems that we forget about the people around us. We don't realize that they suffer with us.

Initially, our friends and loved ones think we will get over the depressed mood. When this does not happen, they begin trying to help. In mild cases this can help but more often than not it doesn't help. This leads to hurt and frustration. Friends and loved ones will blame themselves for failing or begin to distance themselves from the situation.

We must understand that our depressed moods do not put the world on hold. They only put our individual lives on hold. The world and the lives of others go on. The events that continue in the lives of our loved ones include situations where they need us. They need our love and support for the major and minor struggles of life.

We must be there for our friends and loved ones. We must be strong, put our own self-pity aside, and focus on the needs of others. This may mean immediately sucking it up and being tough, or admitting the need for and seeking professional help to first stabilize ourselves, before helping others.

My earlier suggestions included helping people who will never know who helped them, helping children and other individuals. These activities should be distributed between strangers, friends, and loved ones. Don't focus on those you do not know and ignore those who love and support you.

There are many famous quotes that relate that it is not what happens to you in life that makes you who you are, but how you react to what happens to you that makes you who you are. This is true. It is especially true for those who are pessimistic and depressed. It is always appropriate for us to care for and help other people as they need us, and by helping ourselves to assure that we do not become a self-absorbed self-pitying burden upon them.

CHAPTER 50
Read this Book Again

> **Repetition is the mother of all learning.**
>
> ~ *Zig Ziglar*

It does not take long to read this book from beginning to end. However, it may take a week or two to work through each of the recommended activities and probably a full year to complete them all. While you are working through the activities, you should reread the book to reinforce the ideas in your mind and keep your focus. The list of activities in Appendix A will also help you keep your focus.

I have several books and tape series that I have read or listened to multiple times. Each time I feel I gain deeper understanding of the materials. This reinforces my knowledge and makes application of the materials easier and more likely. I benefit from each reading or listening; you can do the same with this book and others you discover.

All right, back to square one you go.

Appendix A
Happy-To-Do List

The following "To Do" list is a collection of the actions recommended in each chapter. Each item can typically be completed or be well on the path to completion within two weeks. Work your way through the list one item at a time. By the time you are half way through the book, I expect that you will see a noticeable difference in your level of happiness.

Appendix B provides an example of a Goal-Planning Worksheet that is recommended for use with each of the activities described in this book. The Worksheet can also be used for any project or goal in life. Photocopy the sheet from the book or reproduce it on your own word processor.

Beginning
- Admit to yourself you are not happy.

- Commit to working toward being happy.

- Begin working on the activities listed here in order to increase the levels of eustress in your life.

- Seek help from a career counselor or mental health professional in identifying your intellectual strengths and your major personality type through the Myers-Briggs Type Indicator.

- Win where you have always lost by studying a topic or activity you have always felt you could not do; then get started doing it.

- Get ready, fire, and then aim at the activity you select in Chapter 4.

- Visit a funeral director and plan your funeral. Become conscious that the clock is ticking.

- Lift your spirits by making a recording or uploading your favorite songs and sing along with it.

- Watch Jerry Springer or a similar program in order to realize your life isn't as bad as you think.

- Start saving $1000.00 for an emergency fund and also begin saving for something you need or want that costs $500.00 or less.

- Start or rejuvenate a hobby.

- Make your hobby or hobbies a life-long activity. Don't delay it until retirement.

- Find something to look forward to.

- Select an unfinished project and finish it.

- Say "No" to the next few requests for time from your already burdened schedule.

- Give up something. Pick an activity or a possession you no longer want or need.

- Find your spot, a place of your very own.

- If needed, get professional help from a mental health professional.

- Teach, coach, mentor, or tutor someone.

- Help someone anonymously.

- Learn something new. Pick a hobby or trade.

- Start listening to educational and motivational audio programs while you drive.

- Take a break from the educational and motivational audio programs by listening to humorous audio programs occasionally.

- Plan two vacations this year. Make sure they are an equal mixture of activity and rest.

- Stop procrastinating and start something, anything.

- Start using goal-action plans, major to-do lists, and daily lists to guide you through your day and week.

- Dress better. Plan what you are going to wear each week.

- Plan your accessories, polish your shoes, and get your hair done.

- Look your best.

- Limit giving to what you can give without expecting anything in return.

- Do the most dreaded, unpleasant tasks first to get them over with.

- Make a list of the positive factors currently in your life.

- Make a list of all positive events and successes from your life to date and continue to develop the list as life continues.

- Reduce your contact with negative news and information from the mass media.

- Take a backpack trip.

- Select an idea you have delayed acting on and put it into action.

- Honor someone who has had a positive influence in your life.

- Stay busy working on positive projects and activities.

- Do not allow yourself to be idle in order to avoid worrying, imagining the worst, and focusing on any health problems you may have.

- Pay attention to the interests, desires, hobbies, and dreams of those you love; and begin to take note of what you can provide to made these interests, desires, hobbies, and dreams easier to participate in or become realities.

- Be a good gift giver.

- Make your own luck by planning your life and setting goals.

- Use the Goal Planning Worksheet in Appendix B to plan the completion of the actions recommended in this book and for setting your other goals.

- Regardless of your age, get out, learn something new, and live.

- Select rewards for reaching the halfway point in this book and for finishing this book.

- Plan and participate in a goofy/adventurous activity or event.

- Know the final score.

- Find a personal trainer and exercise.

- Study your heroes. Pay attention to their extraordinary use of their intelligences while keeping their ordinary characteristics, personality quirks, and faults in perspective.

- Do something for a needy child; there are plenty out there. Buy school supplies or volunteer at a hospital or school.

- Do something for the elderly. Visit a nursing home. Just sit and chat. If you play an instrument, entertain them.

- Learn to recognize the things in your life that trigger good and bad emotions. It will help you avoid the negatives and decrease mood swings

- Challenge yourself to solve a problem by working from the end backwards.

- Make a list of things you regret in your life and work on tempering the effects the regrets have on you.

- Get rid of the clutter in your life. Have a yard sale, give things to the poor, or just go to the dump. Then start collecting experiences instead of stuff.

- Realize the effect your moods and reactions to life have on others and help them by helping yourself with this book and by other means.

- Read this book again.

Appendix B
Goal Planning Worksheet

1. Goal: _____

2. Why:

   _____

   _____

3. Starting Date: _____

4. Completion Date: _____

5. Skills/Resources Needed:

   _____

   _____

6. People/Organizations:

   _____

   _____

7. Obstacles:

   _____

   _____

   _____

8. Action Steps:

   _____

   _____

   _____

   _____

Action Plan Continued:

_____

_____

_____

_____

_____

_____

_____

_____

_____

_____

_____

_____

_____

_____

_____

_____

_____

_____

_____

_____

_____

_____

_____

_____

_____

_____

_____

About the Author

Dr. K. Jeffrey Miller is a native of Shelby County, Kentucky. He received his Bachelor of Science and Doctor of Chiropractic degrees from Palmer College of Chiropractic in Davenport, Iowa in 1987. After graduation he completed postdoctoral orthopedic training through Parker College of Chiropractic in Dallas, Texas. In 1993 Dr. Miller became the first chiropractic orthopedic specialist to practice full-time in the state of Kentucky and was the youngest chiropractic orthopedist in the country. He is both a Diplomat of the American Board of Chiropractic Orthopedist (DABCO) and a Fellow of the Academy of Chiropractic Orthopedist (FACO).

In 1997 Dr. Miller completed boards given by the National Strength and Conditioning Association (NSCA) for designation as a Certified Strength and Conditioning Specialist (CSCS). He also holds personal trainer certifications with the NSCA and the American Council on Exercise. In 2002 he completed coursework and boards for the Certified Chiropractic Sports Practitioner (CCSP) program.

In seventeen years of private practice Dr. Miller published more than a hundred articles in thirty publications and wrote three books: *On-The-Job C.A.R.E.*, a manual on occupational health consulting (three editions), *Practical Assessment of the Chiropractic Patient* (2002), and *Practicing Chiropractic* (2005).

Following private practice Dr. Miller published his fourth and fifth books: *Stat Spinal Examination: How to Examine a Patient Who is Paralyzed by Spasm or Writhing in Pain* (2006) and *The Insurance Game: Winning the Battle for Reimbursement* (2006).

Five of the nation's largest chiropractic colleges have appointed Dr. Miller to their postgraduate faculties as an instructor in orthopedics and occupational health. He was a feature speaker for over a decade for Kats Management Services (now Integrity Management) in Lincoln, Nebraska.

In 2002 Dr. Miller was honored by Business First Magazine as one of the top forty business professionals in the Louisville Metropolitan Area under the age of forty (*the forty under forty* award).

Dr. Miller has served as an assistant professor of structure and function at Palmer College of Chiropractic in Port Orange, Florida and Chairmanship of The Department of Clinical Sciences at Cleveland Chiropractic College in Kansas City, Missouri-Overland Park, Kansas.

Recently Dr. Miller published a set of study flash cards published by Lippincott, Williams and Wilkins/Wolters-Kluwer, *Orthopedic and Neurological Examination in a Flash*. The cards cover 240 of the most useful orthopedic and neurological tests for day-to-day chiropractic practice.

Dr. Miller and his wife Kim have four children: Ben, Andy, Emily, and Katie. They reside in Roanoke, Virginia.

Dr. Miller is available for motivational speaking engagements. Please visit his website at examdoc.com and email him at jeff@examdoc.com.

Robert D. Reed Publishers Order Form

Call in your order for fast service and quantity discounts
(541) 347- 9882

OR order on-line at **www.rdrpublishers.com** *using PayPal.*
OR order by mail:
Make a copy of this form; enclose payment information:
Robert D. Reed Publishers
1380 Face Rock Drive, Bandon, OR 97411
Fax at (541) 347-9883

Send indicated books to:

Name_____

Address _____

City _____ State _____ Zip _____

Phone _____ Fax _____ Cell _____

E-Mail_____

Payment by check ☐ or credit card ☐ *(All major credit cards are accepted.)*

Name on card _____

Card Number _____

Exp. Date _____ Last 3-Digit number on back of card_____

<u>*Qty.*</u>

The Road to Happiness Is Always Under Construction
by K. Jeffrey Miller...$11.95 _____

Fearless by Steve Chandler...$12.95 _____

The New American Prosperity by Darby Checketts ....$12.95 _____

Why Am I So Damned Unhappy? by Jim Downton................$11.95 _____

Running Home by Toby Estler...$14.95 _____

Wisdom is the Answer—Common Sense is the Way
by James Giambrone, Jr. ....$14.95 _____

PICK ONE: Ways You Can Help…
by Colin Ingram & Robert D. Reed ....$14.95 _____

30 Days to a New You by Monica Magnetti ....$19.95 _____

How Bad Do You Really Want It? by Tom Massey ....$19.95 _____

Total Number of Books _____ Total Amount _____

Note: Shipping is $3.50 1st book + $1 for each additional book.   Shipping _____

THE TOTAL____